GOLF
TALK

GOLF TALK

The Greatest Things Ever Said About the Game of Golf

Collected and Selected by Michael Flanders

click
B O O K S

GOLF TALK
The Greatest Things Ever Said About the Game of Golf
ISBN 0-9644693-0-8

Click Books
P.O. Box 4551
North Hollywood, CA 91617-0551

INTRODUCTION

WHAT IS IT ABOUT THE GAME of golf? What is it that has inspired so many words and thoughts? Seemingly, it is a very simple game: Hit a small white ball into a slightly larger hole. What elevates that simple act and transforms golf into the most talked about, most written about, and most thought about of all games? Just what are the mysterious allures that have inspired the passions of so many for so long?

While these questions can never be fully answered — for there are probably as many answers to why golf is such a special game as there are golfers — I hope this selection of thoughts will convey to readers the endless variety of attractions the game offers. This collection spans hundreds of years and the thoughts contained are attributed to a remarkably wide cross-section of people, golfers and non-golfers alike. What they all have in common is that they celebrate, in one way or another, the magic of golf.

I hope you enjoy them.

Michael Flanders

If, AS THE POET SAID, 'Life is a game,'
then it is a game played much better and
more rewardingly because several centuries ago a group of simple Scotsmen,
with perhaps unwitting wisdom saw
the joy to be derived and the lessons
to be learned by combining a stick and
a pellet, the challenges of terrain and
nature, and a hole in the ground.

-Roy Benjamin

IF I EVER NEEDED an eight-foot putt and everything I owned depended on it, I would want Arnold Palmer to putt it for me.

-Bobby Jones

I'M HITTING THE WOODS just great. But I'm having a terrible time hitting out of them.

-Harry Toscano

THE ONLY SURE WAY to get a par is to leave a four-foot putt two inches short of the hole.

-Mulligan's Laws

ON THE GOLF COURSE, a man may be the dogged victim of inexorable fate, be struck down by an appalling stroke of tragedy, become the hero of unbelievable melodrama, or the clown in a side-splitting comedy — any of these within a few hours, and all without having to bury a corpse or repair a tangled personality.

-Robert Tyre Jones

GOLF IS TEMPORARY INSANITY practiced in a pasture.

-Dave Kindred

GOLF IS A GAME whose aim is to hit
a very small ball into a very small hole,
with weapons singularly ill-designed for
the purpose.

-Winston Churchill

AN IDEAL OR CLASSICAL golf course
demands variety, personality, and above
all, the charm of romance.

-Charles Blair Macdonald

GIVE ME A MAN with big hands, big feet,
and no brains and I will make a golfer
out of him.

-Walter Hagen

In COMPETITION, DURING GUNFIRE or while bombs are falling, players may take cover without penalty for ceasing play. The positions of known delayed-action bombs are marked by red flags at a reasonably, but not guaranteed, safe distance therefrom ... A ball moved by enemy action may be replaced, or if lost or 'destroyed' a ball may be dropped not nearer the hole without penalty. A player whose stroke is affected by the simultaneous explosion of a bomb may play another ball from the same place. Penalty, one stroke.

-Temporary Rules, Richmond Golf Club (1940)

GOLF: A GAME IN WHICH a ball one and a half inches in diameter is placed on a ball 8,000 miles in diameter. The object is to hit the small ball but not the larger.

-John Cunningham

I HAD TO TAKE THE BOY aside and teach him how to throw a club. He was so innocent he'd toss them backwards. I had to explain that you'd get worn out walking back to pick them up. You have to throw them in front of you if you're going to be a professional.

-Tommy Bolt
Advice to a young Arnold Palmer

IN SCOTLAND HE IS AS MUCH of an institution as the player himself. He has grown up on the links, and is the guide, counselor, and friend of the player whose clubs he carries. One of his principal qualifications there is that he should be able to conceal his contempt for your game.

-Henry E. Howland
On the caddie, Scribner's Magazine (1895)

EVEN HIS BAD SHOTS are good. That's the secret of golf.

-Johnny Miller
On Fred Couples

ANYTIME YOU GET THE URGE to golf,
instead take 18 minutes and beat your
head against a good solid wall. This
is guaranteed to duplicate to a tee the
physical and emotional beating you
would have suffered playing a round
of golf. If 18 minutes aren't enough,
go for 27 or 36 — whatever feels right.

-Mark Oman

THE GREEDY GOLFER will go too near
and be sucked into his own destruction.

-John Low (1902)

IF YOU PLAY POORLY one day, forget it. If you play poorly the next time out, review your fundamentals of grip, stance, aim, and ball position. Most mistakes are made before the club is swung. If you play poorly for a third time in a row, go see your professional.

-Harvey Penick

THIS PUTT LOOKS slightly straight.

-Mad Mac
Legendary Scottish caddie

I PLAY THIS GAME BECAUSE my sole ambition is to do well enough to give it up.

-David Feherty
On the pressures of professional golf

GOLF IS THE CRUELEST of sports. Like life, it's unfair. It's a harlot. A trollop. It leads you on. It never lives up to its promises. It's not a sport, it's bondage. An obsession. A boulevard of broken dreams. It plays with men. And runs off with the butcher.

-Jim Murray

ARNOLD, THAT'S A BAG full of indecision.

-Jack Burke, Sr.
*To Arnold Palmer, when Palmer arrived
on a practice green with a golf bag
full of putters*

OBVIOUSLY A DEER ON THE FAIRWAY has seen you tee off before and knows that the safest place to be when you play is right down the middle.

-Jackie Gleason
To writer Milton Gross

PUTTING GREENS ARE TO GOLF courses what faces are to portraits.

-Charles Blair Macdonald

IN ALMOST ALL OTHER GAMES you pit yourself against a mortal foe; in golf it is yourself against the world. No human being stays your progress as you drive your ball over the face of the globe.

-Arnold Haultain

I'D LIKE TO SEE THE FAIRWAYS more narrow. Then everybody would have to play from the rough, not just me.

-Seve Ballesteros

IT'S NOT A GIMME if you're still away.

-Mulligan's Laws

WHAT A STUPID I am.

-Roberto de Vicenzo
After learning he had lost the 1968 Masters
for signing an incorrect scorecard

A GOOD GOLF COURSE is like good music or good anything else. It is not necessarily a good course which appeals the first time one plays it, but one which grows on the player the more frequently they visit it.

-Dr. Alister Mackenzie (1920)

IN THE FIELDS CALLED THE LINKS, the citizens of Edinburgh divert themselves at a game called Golf, in which they use a curious kind of bats tipped with horn, and small elastic balls of leather, stuffed with feathers . . . These they strike with such force and dexterity from one hole to another, that they will fly to an incredible distance. Of this diversion the Scots are so fond that, when the weather will permit, you may see a multitude of all ranks, from the senator of justice to the lowest tradesman, mingled together, in their shirts, and following the balls with the utmost eagerness. Among others, I was shown one particular set of golfers, the youngest of whom was turned four-score. They were all gentlemen of independent fortunes, who had amused themselves with this pastime for the best part of a century, without ever having felt the least alarm from sickness or disgust; and they never went to bed without having each the best part of a gallon of claret in his belly. Such uninterrupted exercise, co-operating with the keen air from the sea, must, without all doubt, keep the appetite always on edge, and steel the constitution against all the common attacks of distemper.

-Tobis Smollet (1721-1771)
From Humphrey Clinker

THE SECRET OF GOLF is to turn three shots into two.

-Bobby Jones

THE ESSENCE OF GOLF is more than a game; it's a philosophy of life. In life as well as in golf we must maintain a state of balance between rest and activity.

-Link St. Clair
Quantum Golf *by Kjell Enhager*

LIKE THE CLASSIC plays and symphonies, Sam Snead doesn't belong to just one generation. His mark will be left on golf for an eternity.

-Peter Thomson

IF JIMMY HAD CONCENTRATED on golf
as much as laughing and making people
laugh, he might have won more tournaments. Of course, I wouldn't have liked
him as much.

-Ben Hogan
On Jimmy Demaret

ANYONE WHO CRITICIZES a golf course
is like a person invited to a house for
dinner who, on leaving, tells the host
that the food was lousy.

-Gary Player

PICK UP THE BALL, have the clubs destroyed, and leave the course.

-Viscount Castlerosse
British columnist, to his caddie,
after topping three straight shots

THE PERSON I FEAR most in the last two rounds is myself.

-Tom Watson

IF YOU PICK UP A GOLFER and hold him close to your ear, like a conch shell, and listen, you will hear an alibi.

-Fred Beck

SUCCESS IN THIS GAME depends less on strength of body than strength of mind and character.

-Arnold Palmer

I HAVE COME TO THINK that a person grows in his regard for the rules as he improves his game. The best players come to love golf so much they hate to see it violated in any way.

-Michael Murphy
Author, Golf in the Kingdom

You've just one problem. You stand too close to the ball — after you've hit it.

-Sam Snead
To a student

If that all-important rule, Keep your Eye upon the Ball, means anything at all, it means to keep it on the ball so that the ball is distinctly seen and attended to. One should watch one's ball as a cat watches a mouse. No cat watches a mouse with downcast eyes or with a vacant stare; and no cat, while it watches a mouse, is thinking of anything else.

-Arnold Haultain

A GOOD PART OF THE AVERAGE golfer's difficulty comes from the understandable desire and effort to do more than he can. The determination to get length at any cost, to use the strongest club possible, more often than not leads him to exceed his limit.

-Bobby Jones

THE GAME OF GOLF is 90% mental and 10% mental.

-Mulligan's Laws

THAT PUTT WAS SO GOOD, I could feel
the baby applaud.

-Donna Horton-White
After sinking a long putt
while seven months pregnant

THERE'S NOTHING WRONG with the
St. Andrews course that 100 bulldozers
couldn't put right. The Old Course needs
a dry clean and press.

-Ed Furgol

THE SPICE OF GOLF, as of life, lies in variety.

-Robert Hunter

NOT ONLY DID JIMMY never practice, I don't think he ever slept.

-Sam Snead
On Jimmy Demaret

NOW HERE'S JACK LEMMON, about to play an all-important eighth shot.

-Jim McKay
*Reporting from the 14th hole
at the 1959 Crosby at Pebble Beach*

DONA' WORRY ABOUT THE SCORE so much, it's not the important thing.

-Shivas Irons
Golf in the Kingdom *by Michael Murphy*

THE MOST EXQUISITELY satisfying act in the world of golf is that of throwing a club. The full backswing, the delayed wrist action, the flowing follow-through, followed by that unique whirring sound, reminiscent only of a passing flock of starlings, are without parallel in sport.

-Henry Longhurst

WHAT OTHER PEOPLE MAY FIND in poetry or art museums, I find in the flight of a good drive.

-Arnold Palmer

WHEN TEACHING OR LEARNING what is wrong with a swing, first decide if the thing to work on is the swing itself or the angle of the clubface at impact.

-Harvey Penick

THE MAN LOOKS LIKE a jukebox with feet. In fact, even his feet look like jukeboxes.

-Tommy Bolt
On Doug Sanders' sartorial style

You ARE A FORTUNATE PERSON, indeed, if you can begin each day accepting the fact that during that day there will be ups and downs, good breaks and bad ones, disappointments, surprises, unexpected turns of events. At the same time wise golfers have learned to accept those adverse conditions on the golf course as representative of real life challenges.

-Roy Benjamin

IN PLAYING A PITCH, chip, or shot from a bunker near the green, there is one significant difference to be noted between the method of the expert player and that of the duffer; in one case, the swing is amply long, smooth, and unhurried; in the other, it is short and jerky, because the club has not been swung back far enough.

-Bobby Jones

I CALL MY SAND WEDGE my 'half-Nelson,' because I can always strangle the opposition with it.

-Byron Nelson

GOLF COMBINES TWO FAVORITE American pastimes: Taking long walks and hitting things with a stick.

-P. J. O'Rourke

I DON'T CARE WHAT ANYBODY SAYS. The first tournament is not the hardest one to win. It's always the second one.

-John Daly

HE ENJOYS THAT PERFECT PEACE, that peace beyond all understanding, which comes at its maximum only to the man who has given up golf.

-P. G. Wodehouse

GOLF CLUBS AREN'T ONLY TOOLS. They're totems. The game turns on illusions.

-Frank Hannigan

GOLF IS A BLOODLESS SPORT if you don't count ulcers.

-Dick Schaap

IT'S THE ONLY IRON we have left.

-Tommy Bolt's caddie
When the club-throwing pro asked
why he was handed a two-iron
for a seven-iron shot

IF YOU REALLY WANT TO GET better at golf, go back and take it up at a much earlier age.

-Mulligan's Laws

IF YOU CAN'T BREAK 80, you have no business playing golf. If you can break 80, you have no business.

-Old British saying

GOLF MAKES LIARS out of honest men, cheats out of altruists, cowards out of brave men, and fools out of everybody.

-Milton Gross

A SICK APPENDIX IS NOT AS DIFFICULT to deal with as a five-foot putt.

-Gene Sarazen

A ROUND OF GOLF should permit eighteen inspirations.

-A. W. Tillinghast

THE HARDEST SHOT IS A MASHIE at ninety yards from the green, where the ball has to be played against an oak tree, bounced back into a sand trap, hits a stone, bounces on the green, and then rolls into the cup. That shot is so difficult I have only made it once.

-Zeppo Marx

LET'S JUST SAY THAT I WALK to a different set of sprinkler heads.

-Greg Ritz, caddie
On the difference between working for Curtis Strange and the long-hitting John Daly

REALLY GOOD GOLF HOLES are full of surprises, each one a bit better than the last.

-Robert Hunter

IF YOUR CADDIE COACHES YOU on the tee, 'Hit it down the left side with a little draw,' ignore him. All you do on the tee is try not to hit the caddie.

-Jim Murray

TAKE DEAD AIM.

-Harvey Penick

To CONTROL HIS OWN BALL, all alone without help or hindrance, the golfer must first and last entirely control himself, and himself only. The little round toy sitting so alone and so still, which has so fascinated and tantalized the human animal for more than five centuries, is thus uniquely a psychic as well as physical cynosure of muscular skill and mental concentration.

-John Stuart Martin

ANYONE WHO HOPES to reduce putting — or any other department of the game of golf for that matter — to an exact science, is in for a serious disappointment, and will only suffer from the attempt.

-Bobby Jones

I STILL SWING THE WAY I USED TO, but when I look up the ball is going in a different direction.

-Lee Trevino

THE GOLF SWING is like a suitcase into which we are trying to pack one too many items.

-John Updike

GOLF IS A GAME that must always be uncertain. I don't believe that anyone will ever master it to the extent that several have mastered billiards or chess. If someone should do so, I think he would give it up — but that is a danger most of us would be willing to risk.

-Bobby Jones

CAN YOU SEE THE BROOK that golfers fear and not fearing, but feeling, can you put that flowing water into your swing?

-Shivas Irons
Golf in the Kingdom *by Michael Murphy*

I SAY, DO YOU CHAPS actually try to play this hole or do you simply photograph it and go on?

-Eustace Storey
*British player from the 1920's,
on the punishing second hole
at Pine Valley*

EVERY KID LEARNING HOW TO PLAY golf dreams about winning the Masters, about winning the Open, not about being the leading money winner. I've never short-changed myself on dreams.

-Tom Kite

IF THE WIND IS IN YOUR FACE, you swing
too hard just to get the ball through it;
if the wind is at your back, you swing too
hard just to see how far you can get the
ball to go.

-Mulligan's Laws

THERE ARE THREE WAYS of learning golf:
By study, which is the most wearisome;
by imitation, which is the most fallacious;
and by experience, which is the most bitter.

-Robert Browning

KEEP ON HITTING IT STRAIGHT until the
wee ball goes in the hole.

-James Braid

FAIRWAY: A NARROW STRIP of mown grass that separates two groups of golfers looking for lost balls in the rough.

-Henry Beard and Roy McKie

IF YOU COULD BOTTLE nervous energy and use it at the right time, you could hit shots you didn't think you were capable of hitting.

-Nick Price

CLOSE IN GOLF USUALLY MEANS one more putt.

-Bob Murphy

THE DIFFERENCE BETWEEN GOLF and government is that in golf you can't improve your lie.

-George Deukmejian
Former Governor of California

REAL GOLFERS GO TO WORK to relax.

-George Dillon

GOLF IS JUST A GAME, and an idiotic one at that.

-Mark Calcavecchia
After failing to make the cut at a British Open

THE BEST SINGLE PIECE of advice I could give any man starting out for a round of golf would be 'take your time,' not in studying the ground, and lining up the shot, but in swinging the club.

-Bobby Jones

I'D RATHER PLAY GOLF and break even, than work hard and come out ahead.

-Mike Donald

CYPRESS POINT HAS JUST COMPLETED a highly successful membership drive. Forty members resigned.

-Bob Hope
On Monterey's ultra-exclusive Cypress Point

THERE ISN'T A 7-IRON shot at Merion.

-Ben Hogan
When reporters asked him
why he didn't carry a 7-iron
in his bag when he won
the 1950 U.S. Open at Merion

I KNOW I'M GETTING BETTER at golf because I'm hitting fewer spectators.

-Former President Gerald Ford

IF YOU'RE GOING TO MISS 'EM, miss 'em quick.

-George Duncan
1920 British Open champion, on putting

THERE ARE GUYS WHO ARE respected for their long games, and guys who are respected for their short games. But there are also guys who win respect because they know the golf swing and have the ability, even when playing poorly, to make something happen.

-Nick Price

GOLF, LIKE MEASLES, should be caught young, for, if postponed to riper years, the results may be serious.

-P. G. Wodehouse

Billy Munn, ONE OF MY BETTER college players, came into the golf shop at Austin Country Club and said he was putting poorly. He asked if I would help.

When we left the shop, Billy walked toward the practice green and I walked toward the practice range.

He thought I misunderstood.

'Hey, Mr. Penick!' he yelled. 'It's my putting that needs looking at!'

'Billy, you're a good putter,' I yelled back. 'If you aren't having success, it's because your iron shots are too far from the hole.'

-Harvey Penick

YOU'LL NEVER LEARN TO PLAY GOLF on a golf course. The place to learn how to play golf is on the practice range.

-Lee Trevino

NOBODY WINS THE OPEN, it wins you.

-Dr. Cary Middlecoff
On the U.S. Open

KEEP ON HITTING THE BALL no matter what happens.

-Harry Vardon

PEOPLE SHOULD NOT LOSE TRACK of the simple fact that it's the club head that hits the ball. You've got to learn to have a relationship with the club head, to know where it's going and what it's doing, and how it's positioned throughout the swing. But most of all, most of all, you've got to feel the club.

-Jim Flick

PUTTING ISN'T GOLF. Greens should be treated almost the same as water hazards: You land on them, then add two strokes to your score.

-Chi Chi Rodriguez

No MATTER HOW HARD I TRY, I just can't seem to break sixty-four.

-Jack Nicklaus

IF GOLF IS BASICALLY A TEST of nerve, a two-dollar Nassau is essentially a concentration aid.

-Tom Callahan

BAD PUTTING IS DUE MORE to the effect the green has upon the player than it has upon the action of the ball.

-Bobby Jones

TOMMY BOLT'S PUTTER has more air time than Lindbergh.

-Jimmy Demaret

THE TRUE GOLFER IS CRITICAL of lucky strokes or flukes; in his estimation they are as discreditable as bad ones; certainty and precision is his standard, and his comment in broad Scotch, the real golf language, after a bad shot by a good player, calculated to draw applause from ignorant bystanders, would probably be, 'My, but yon was a lucky yin, bad play — didna desairve it.'

-Henry E. Howland
Scribner's Magazine (1895)

NOTHING DISSECTS A MAN in public quite like golf.

-Brent Musberger

INDEED, THE HIGHEST PLEASURE of golf may be that on the fairways and far from all the pressures of commerce and rationality, we can feel immortal for a few hours.

-Colman McCarthy

NO MATTER HOW SHORT the par three, the drive is never a gimme.

-Mulligan's Laws

WHEREIN DO THE CHARMS of this game lie, that captivate youth, and retain their hold till far on in life? . . . It is a fine, open-air, athletic exercise, not violent, but bringing into play nearly all the muscles of the body; while that exercise can be continued for hours. It is a game of skill, needing mind and thought and judgement, as well as a cunning hand. It is also a social game, where one may go out with one friend or with three, as the case may be, and enjoy mutual intercourse, mingled with an excitement which is very pleasing . . . It never palls or grows stale, as morning by morning the players appear at the teeing-ground with as keen a relish as if they had not seen a club for a month. Nor is it only while the game lasts that the zest is felt. How the player loves to recall the strokes and other incidents of the match, so that it is often played over again next morning while still in bed!

-James Balfour (1887)

IF I'VE LEARNED ONE THING about the game it is that 'tis many things to many people, includin' the many ones in my very own head.

-Peter McNaughton
Golf in the Kingdom *by Michael Murphy*

NO WAY. GOLF'S too boring.

-Greg Norman's daughter Morgan-Leigh
*On whether she wants to follow
in her fathers footsteps and become
a professional golfer*

MORE OFTEN THAN NOT, the first impression in golf is the best. There is no man capable of hitting a golf ball with sufficient exactness to warrant concern about the minute undulations a very close examination might reveal. If he can care for the difficulties he can see at a glance, he will have done well enough.

-Bobby Jones

Be YOUR OWN BEST FRIEND. There may not be a more important mental factor in golf than this. There are enough challenges in the course of the game that try our character. The last thing we need is to be our own judge, jury, and executioner. If we are going to talk to ourselves on the course, and we all do, let that conversation be supportive and positive.

-The PGA Manual of Golf

Golf is not a wrestle with Bogey;
it is not a struggle with your mortal foe,
it is a physiological, psychological, and
moral fight with yourself; it is a test of
mastery over self; and the ultimate and
irreducible element of the game is to
determine which of the players is the
more worthy combatant.

-Arnold Haultain

GOLF INCREASES THE BLOOD pressure, ruins the disposition, spoils the digestion, induces neurasthenia, hurts the eyes, callouses the hands, ties kinks in the nervous system, debauches the morals, drives men to drink or homicide, breaks up the family, turns the ductless glands into internal warts, corrodes the pneumo-gastric nerve, breaks off the edges of the vertebrae, induces spinal meningitis and progressive mendacity, and starts angina pectoris.

-Dr. A. S. Lamb (early 1900's)

EVERY YEAR I PLAYED golf, I discovered more and more ways to miss shots, obscure and yet important mistakes I had never dreamed of making.

-Bobby Jones

IF YOU WATCH A GAME, it's fun. If you play it, it's recreation. If you work at it, it's golf.

-Bob Hope

I HAVE LOVED PLAYING the game and practicing it. Whether my schedule for the following day called for a tournament round or merely a trip to the practice tee, the prospect that there was going to be golf in it made me feel privileged and extremely happy. I couldn't wait for the sun to come up so that I could get out on the course again.

-Ben Hogan

GOLFERS PLAY GOLF to prove that they can mentally overcome the pressures that golf puts upon them. The fact that if they didn't play golf at all they would not have to endure or overcome its pressures may not occur to them.

-Peter Gammond

EIGHTEEN HOLES OF MATCH play will teach you more about your foe than nineteen years of dealing with him across a desk.

-Grantland Rice

PROBABLY THE WORST HOLE on the course. Then again, being the worst hole at Pebble is like being the ugliest Miss America.

-Rick Reilly
On the 11th hole at Pebble Beach

THE PLAYER MAY EXPERIMENT about his swing, his grip, his stance. It is only when he begins asking his caddie's advice that he is getting on dangerous ground.

-Sir Walter Simpson

I NEVER SAW BYRON NELSON play, and I've only seen Ben Hogan hit balls, but I've played a lot with Sam, and he plays the game the way it's supposed to be played — the way you dream about playing just once in your life.

-Ben Crenshaw
On Sam Snead

KEEP YOUR EYE ON THE CLUB. Nothing is more embarrassing than to throw a club and then have to ask a playing partner where it went.

-Glen Waggoner
On club-throwing etiquette

GOLF IS A WAY OF TESTING ourselves while enjoying ourselves.

-Arnold Palmer

ALL MEN ARE CREATED EQUAL and I am one shot better than the rest.

-Gene Sarazen

IF YOU HAVE A BAD GRIP, you don't want a good swing.

-Harvey Penick

GIVE ME GOLF CLUBS, the fresh air, and a beautiful partner, and you can keep my golf clubs and the fresh air.

-Jack Benny

IT TOOK ME SEVENTEEN YEARS to get three thousand hits in baseball. I did it in one afternoon on the golf course.

-Hank Aaron

WE BORROWED GOLF from Scotland as we borrowed whiskey. Not because it's Scottish, but because it's good.

-Horace G. Hutchinson

THERE'S NO SUCH THING as natural touch. Touch is something you create by hitting millions of golf balls.

-Lee Trevino

GOLF IS THE HARDEST GAME in the world to play, and the easiest to cheat at.

-Dave Hill

I GOT AS MUCH FUN as the next man from whaling a ball as hard as I could and catching it squarely on the button. But from sad experience I learned not to try this in a round that meant anything.

-Bobby Jones

YOU CAN WIN TOURNAMENTS when you're mechanical, but golf is a game of emotion and adjustment. If you're not aware of what's happening to your mind and body when you're playing, you'll never be able to be the very best you can be.

-Jack Nicklaus

THE GAME WAS INVENTED a billion years ago — don't you remember?

-Old Scottish saying

THE GAME CAN BE PLAYED in company or alone. Robinson Crusoe on his island, with his man Friday as a caddie, could have realized the golfer's dream of perfect happiness — a fine day, a good course, and a clear green.

-Henry E. Howland
Scribner's Magazine (1895)

THE GAME IS NOT SO EASY as it seems. In the first place, the terrible *inertia* of the ball must be overcome.

-Lord Wellwood

IF THE AVERAGE AMERICAN PLAYER would only realize how much easier it is to play well when he is swinging along at a good rate, he would surely gird up his loins and walk a little faster.

-H. J. Whigham
The Common Sense of Golf (1910)

YOU HAVE TO MAKE CORRECTIONS in your game a little bit at a time. It's like taking your medicine. A few aspirin will probably cure what ails you, but the whole bottle might just kill you.

-Harvey Penick

GOLF IS THE ONE GAME I know which becomes more and more difficult the longer one plays it.

-Bobby Jones

CLAYTON HEAFNER WAS THE MOST even-tempered golfer I ever saw. He was mad all the time.

-Sam Snead

MY BEST GOLF SCORE is 103, but I've only been playing for 15 years.

-Alex Karras
Football great

CURSED BE THE HAND that made these holes.

-William Shakespeare
Richard III

NEVER BET WITH ANYONE you meet on the first tee who has a deep suntan, a one-iron, and squinty eyes.

-Dave Marr

GOLF IS A GAME WHERE GUTS, stick-to-itiveness and blind devotion will always net you absolutely nothing but an ulcer.

-Tommy Bolt

I'D GIVE UP GOLF if I didn't have so many sweaters.

-Bob Hope

NOTHING HAS CHANGED since caveman days when some Neanderthal in plaid pants first picked up a club and tried to groove an inside-out path. We're all still looking for a repeating swing that works.

-Glen Waggoner

I HAVE A TIP that can take five strokes off anyone's game. It's called an eraser.

-Arnold Palmer

GOLF IS LIKE A LOVE AFFAIR. If you don't take it seriously, it's not any fun. If you take it seriously, it will break your heart.

-Arthur Daly

NOTHING FUNNY EVER HAPPENS at Augusta. Dogs don't bark and babies don't cry. They wouldn't dare.

-Frank Chirkinian,
CBS Sports producer

TOO MUCH AMBITION is a bad thing to have in a bunker.

-Bobby Jones

THE AVERAGE GOLFER doesn't play golf, he attacks it.

-Jackie Burke

IF YOU WERE ASKED to imagine what flavor of ice cream would describe your golf swing, I would like to hear you answer, 'vanilla.' The more simple your approach to the swing is, the better off you are. It's the simple things that last.

-Harvey Penick

HIT 'EM HARD, They'll land somewhere.

-Stewart Maiden (1919)

IF I OWNED A REMBRANDT, I don't think I'd want to go slapping on some reds and yellows just because it was kind of dull.

-Raymond Floyd
*On the 'improvements'
to Oak Hill since 1980*

GOLF APPEALS TO THE IDIOT in us and the child. What child does not grasp the simple pleasure-principle of miniature golf? Just how childlike golf players become is proven by their frequent inability to count past five.

-John Updike

IT'S GOOD SPORTSMANSHIP to not pick up lost golf balls while they're still rolling.

-Mark Twain

IT IS A WONDERFUL TRIBUTE to the game or to the dottiness of the people who play it that for some people somewhere there is no such thing as an insurmountable obstacle, an unplayable course, the wrong time of the day or year.

-Alistair Cooke

GOLF IS A FICKLE GAME, and must be wooed to be won.

-William Park, Jr.

How OFTEN HAVE WE SEEN a round go from an episode of The Three Stooges to the agonies of King Lear - perhaps in the space of one hole! I will never forget a friend who declared after his tee shot that he wanted to kill himself but when the hole was finished, said with total sincerity, that he had never been so happy in his entire life. No other game is capable of evoking a person's total commitment.

-Michael Murphy
Author, Golf in the Kingdom

The SECRET OF MISSING a tree is to aim straight at it.

-Michael Green

WHEN YOU REFLECT on the combination of characteristics that golf demands of those who would presume to play it, it is not surprising that golf has never had a truly great player who was not also a person of extraordinary character.

-Frank D. "Sandy" Tatum, Jr.

THE WAY I PUTTED, I must have been reading the greens in Spanish and putting them in English.

-Homero Blancas

I don't take vacations that long.

-Chi Chi Rodriguez
Watching one of John Daly's drives

WHEN HE GETS THE BALL into a tough place, that's when he's most relaxed. I think it's because he has so much experience at it.

-Don Christopher
Jack Lemmon's caddie

THE MOST IMPORTANT THING for golfers of all ages and handicaps is not that they should play golf well, but that they should play it cheerfully.

-H. J. Whigham
The Common Sense of Golf (1910)

THE MORE TIME I have to think about a shot the worse I'm going to hit it.

-Larry Laoretti

I'M GOING TO MISS at least seven shots
in every 18 holes, so if I'm going to be
angry, I might as well start right on the
first tee.

-Walter Hagen

GIVE ME A MILLIONAIRE with a fast
backswing and I can have a very
enjoyable afternoon.

-George Low

BOB HOPE: Okay, what's wrong with
my game?

ARNOLD PALMER: If you're talking about
golf, that's not your game.

Putting is largely mental, and on this account becomes so difficult. The novice who has not back of him recollections of scores of missed putts a couple of feet or so from the hole is more apt to bring off a putt of this distance, especially on a keen green, than the other fellow. He is not troubled with any thought of being a yard or more away from a miss, and in blissful ignorance confidently bangs away and holes.

-Walter J. Travis (1900)

Hey, what's that? Looks like an old abandoned golf course!

-Sam Snead
On first seeing St. Andrews
by train in 1946

CALL ME OLD-FASHIONED or starchy or whatever you will, but two things in this world I just can't grow accustomed to are a man and a woman living together without being married — and taking a mulligan at golf.

-Harvey Penick

GOLF IS THE MOST OVERTAUGHT and least learned human endeavor. If they taught sex the way they teach golf, the race would have died out years ago.

-Jim Murray

GOLF MAY BE PLAYED on Sunday, not being a game within the view of the law, but being a form of moral effort.

-Stephen Leacock

. . . IF YE CAN ENJOY the walkin', ye can probably enjoy the other times in yer life when ye're in between, and that's most o' the time; wouldn't ye say?

-Shivas Irons
On walking through a round of golf
Golf in the Kingdom *by Michael Murphy*

THE THING WITH GOLF is, it's like a cat chasing its tail. You're never going to catch it. The day you think you've got your swing down pat, something goes awry and you've got to go to the driving range.

-Greg Norman

I ALWAYS LIKE TO SEE a person stand up to a golf ball as though he were perfectly at home in its presence.

-Bobby Jones

GOLF IS A GOOD WALK spoiled.

-Mark Twain

OVER THE YEARS, I've studied habits of golfers. I know what to look for. Watch their eyes. Fear shows up when there is an enlargement of the pupils. Big pupils lead to big scores.

-Sam Snead

IF USGA PEOPLE TOOK OVER the Louvre, they'd paint a mustache on the Mona Lisa.

-Roger Maltbie
*On USGA efforts to make Pebble Beach
more difficult for the 1992 U.S. Open*

KEEP SWINGIN'.

-Shivas Irons
Golf in the Kingdom *by Michael Murphy*

Golf is not a game of great shots. It's a game of the most accurate misses. The people who win make the smallest mistakes.

-Gene Littler

If he elects to take the penalty, his nearest drop is Honolulu.

-Jimmy Demaret
*On the plight of Arnold Palmer's
tee shot on the 17th at
Pebble Beach in 1964*

Your SCORE IN ANY GIVEN round or match is, of course, the measurement of your success in terms of strokes taken. It is your grade on that day's exam. But you do not succeed by thinking solely of your final score any more than you ace a test by answering every question at once. Just like a test, a round of golf must be built a section or a shot at a time. The score is really nothing more than the result of the effort. So next time, don't think score, think only of the shot you have before you and let the final grade take care of itself.

-The PGA Manual of Golf

WHEN YOU TOP A DRIVE into a bunker or miss a short putt at a critical point of the match, remember that you are playing a game for amusement, even if you are desperately keen to win, which you have every right to be. Tell yourself that your only chance of winning lies in forgetting past errors.

-H. J. Whigham
The Common Sense of Golf (1910)

IT IS A WONDERFUL EXPERIENCE to go about a town where people wave at you from doorways and windows, where strangers smile and greet you by name, and where simple and direct courtesy is the outstanding characteristic.

-Bobby Jones
On St. Andrews

THINKING MUST BE THE HARDEST thing we do in golf, because we do so little of it.

-Harvey Penick

Handicap: An allocation of strokes on one or more holes that permits two golfers of very different ability to do equally poorly on the same course.

-Henry Beard and Roy McKie

He plays a game with which I'm not familiar.

-Bobby Jones
After watching Jack Nicklaus
win the 1965 Masters

Nonchalant putts count the same as chalant putts.

-Mulligan's Laws

GOLF IS A GAME BASED not only on an intellectual understanding but also on sensitivity for the instrument. You can't bully your way to a good golf swing.

-Jim Flick

IF I SWUNG THE GAVEL like I swung the golf club, the nation would be in a helluva mess.

-Tip O'Neill
Former Speaker of the House of Representatives

THE RIGHT WAY TO PLAY golf is to go up and hit the bloody thing.

-George Duncan

Don't let the bad shots get to you. Don't let yourself become angry. The true scramblers are thick-skinned. And they always beat the whiners.

-Paul Runyan

The life of a professional golfer is precarious at best. Win and they carry you to the clubhouse on their shoulders; lose and you pay the caddies in the dark.

-Gene Sarazen

Unless you have a reasonably good grip and stance, anything you read about the golf swing is useless.

-Harvey Penick

OH, GOLF IS FOR SMELLIN' heather and cut grass and walkin' fast across the countryside and feelin' the wind and watchin' the sun go down and seein' yer friends hit good shots and hittin' some yerself. It's love and it's feelin' the splendor o' this good world.

-Agatha McNaughton
Golf in the Kingdom *by Michael Murphy*

FOR TWO OR THREE DAYS after I won, I kept calling the number where you can get your bank balance, and I listened to it over and over again.

-Leonard Thompson
After ending a 12-year victory drought

THERE'S ONLY ONE WAY to play the game. You might as well praise a man for not robbing a bank as to praise him for playing by the rules.

-Bobby Jones

NOTHING. ONCE YOU'VE HAD them you've got them.

-Tommy Armour
When asked what one could do to cure 'the yips'

IT IS BETTER TO MISS the shot a hundred times in the right way than to play it successfully in the wrong.

-H. J. Whigham
The Common Sense of Golf (1910)

EVERYBODY HAS THEM, and they always make themselves known on the golf course.

-Bobby Jones
On nerves

THERE WE GO! Miles and miles and miles!

-Astronaut Alan Shepard
Hitting a six-iron on the moon in 1971

IT LOOKS LIKE a slice to me, Al.

-Astronaut Ed Mitchel
As he watched Shepard's shot

WHEN A PRO HITS IT LEFT to right, it's called a fade. When an amateur hits it left to right, it's called a slice.

-Peter Jacobsen

GOLF: A GAME IN WHICH you claim the privileges of age, and retain the playthings of childhood.

-Samuel Johnson

IF WE COULD HAVE SCREWED another head on his shoulders, he would have been the greatest golfer that ever lived.

-Ben Hogan
On Tommy Bolt

WHEN YOUR SHOT has to carry over a water hazard, you can either hit one more club or two more balls.

-Mulligan's Laws

GOLF IS A GAME in which you yell 'fore', shoot six, and write down five.

-Paul Harvey

I'M ONLY SCARED of three things: Lightning, a sidehill putt, and Ben Hogan.

-Sam Snead

HALF THE BATTLE OF GOLF consists of taking it easy. Irritation over a bad shot, anxiety about a bunker in front of you, and especially the effort to drive against a strong wind, may tempt you to hurry your swing. If you give in to the impulse, the result is almost sure to be bad, and the habit of pressing grows on you.

-H. J. Whigham
The Common Sense of Golf (1910)

LOCAL RULES: A set of regulations that are ignored only by the players on one specific course rather than by golfers as a whole.

-Henry Beard and Roy McKie

THE AVERAGE GOLFER, if I am a fair specimen, is hooked when he hits his first good shot; the ball climbs into the air all of its own, it seems — a soaring speck conjured from the effortless airiness of an accidentally correct swing. And then, he or she, that average golfer, spends endless frustrating afternoons, whole decades of them, trying to recover and tame the delicate wildness of the first sweet swing. Was ever any sporting motion so fraught with difficulty and mystery?

-John Updike

IT IS A LAW OF NATURE that everybody plays a hole badly when playing through.

-Bernard Darwin

FOR A WHILE ON THE LINKS we can lord it over our tiny solar system and pretend we are God. No wonder then that we suffer so deeply when our planet goes astray.

-Shivas Irons
On the golf ball
Golf in the Kingdom *by Michael Murphy*

GOLF IS THE MOST FUN you can have without taking your clothes off.

-Chi Chi Rodriguez

THE ONLY THING YOU SHOULD force in a golf swing is the club back into the bag.

-Byron Nelson

I MISS THE HOLE, I miss the hole, I miss the hole, I make it.

-Seve Ballesteros
*On how he four-putted
the 16th green at the
1988 Masters*

THE REAL WAY TO ENJOY playing golf is to take pleasure not in the score, but in the execution of strokes.

-Bobby Jones

GOLF IS FIRST A GAME of seeing and feeling. It can teach you stillness of mind and sensitivity to the textures of wind and green. The best instructional books have always said this. Golf is also a game to teach you about the messages from within, about the subtle voices of the body-mind. And once you understand them you can more clearly see your 'harmatia', the ways in which your approach to the game reflects your entire life. Nowhere does a person go so naked.

-Michael Murphy
Author, Golf in the Kingdom

IT WOULD BE WISE for a tyro not to watch a professional match until he has made a trial himself. 'Can you play the violin?' a boy was asked. 'I don't know,' he replied, 'I never tried;' and the novice at golf, to whom it all looks so easy, would probably make the same answer.

-Henry E. Howland
Scribner's Magazine (1895)

WHEN I MAKE A BAD SHOT, your job is to take the blame.

-Seve Ballesteros
To his caddies

ONE REWARD GOLF HAS GIVEN me, and I shall always be thankful for it, is introducing me to some of the world's most picturesque, tireless, and bald-faced liars.

-Rex Lardner

PEOPLE ARE ALWAYS WONDERING who's better, Hogan or Nicklaus. Well, I've seen Jack Nicklaus watch Ben practice, but I've never seen Ben watch anybody practice. What's that tell you?

-Tommy Bolt

A LONG TIME AGO I asked my teacher what the best exercise was for golf. He said simply, 'Hitting golf balls'.

-Larry Miller

GOLF, TO THE MAN OR WOMAN who regards it simply as a game, will remain forever insoluble and an enigma, and it will retain its greatness because it contains something that lifts it higher than that of a mere pastime.

-J. H. Taylor

THE GREENS WERE TURNING blue
out there.

-Tom Kite
*On final round weather
conditions at the 1992 U.S. Open
at Pebble Beach*

GOLF IS THE ONLY GAME where the
worst player gets the best of it. He
obtains more out of it as regards both
exercise and enjoyment, for the good
player gets worried over the slightest
mistake, whereas the poor player makes
too many mistakes to worry over them.

-David Lloyd George

WHEN I THINK OF AUGUSTA I think of great beauty. I don't know of a golf course where you have such tremendous beauty anywhere in the world. And I've always said that if they have a course like this in heaven I hope I'm the head pro there one day.

-Gary Player
On Augusta National

GOLF IS THE HARDEST GAME in the world. There's no way you can ever get it. Just when you think you do, the game jumps up and puts you in your place.

-Ben Crenshaw

THERE ARE NOW MORE golf clubs in the world than Gideon Bibles, more golf balls than missionaries and, if every golfer in the world, male and female, were laid end to end, I for one would leave them there.

-Michael Parkinson
The Anti-Golf Society

LOOKING UP IS THE BIGGEST alibi ever invented to explain a terrible shot. By the time you look up, you've already made the mistake that caused the bad shot.

-Harvey Penick

NO MATTER WHAT HAPPENS, never give up a hole. To quit between tee and green is more habit-forming than drinking a highball before breakfast.

-Sam Snead

IT'S A SHAME, but he'll never make a golfer. Too much temper.

-Alex Smith
Golf pro, on then 13-year old
Bobby Jones

LIKE CHESS, GOLF IS a game that is for-ever challenging but cannot be conquered.

-Harvey Penick

IT WAS TIME for the club to die.

-Ken Green
*Touring pro, when asked
why he tossed his putter in a lake*

SOMETHING OUGHT TO BE DONE to stop this creeping paralysis which is coming over the game. Most of the delay is quite avoidable. No good player was ever a slow player. Some are faster than others, but I have never seen a good golfer who could not easily get around in two hours with a clear green. If the dawdlers only knew it, they would play a far better game if they would give up dawdling.

-H. J. Whigham
The Common Sense of Golf (1910)

VERY OFTEN WHAT A MAN feels he is doing is more important than what he does. The feel, the experience, is so much easier to remember and repeat.

-Bobby Jones

TO GET AN ELEMENTARY GRASP of the game of golf, you must learn, by endless practice, a continuous and subtle series of highly unnatural movements, involving sixty-four muscles, that result in a seem-ingly 'natural' swing, taking all of two seconds to begin and end.

-Alistair Cooke

TRENT, I'VE JUST SEEN A COURSE you'd really like. You stand on the first tee and take an unplayable lie.

-Jimmy Demaret
To course designer Robert Trent Jones

THE NICE THING ABOUT these golf books is that they usually cancel each other out. One book tells you to keep your eye on the ball; the next says not to bother. Personally, in the crowd I play with, a better idea is to keep your eye on your partner.

-Jim Murray

THE FASCINATIONS OF GOLF can only be learned by experience. It is difficult to explain them. It has its humorous and its serious side. It can be begun as soon as you can walk, and once begun it is continued as long as you can see.

-Henry E. Howland
Scribner's Magazine (1895)

THE WRISTS PLAY VERY LITTLE part in golf. The crossing of the forearms puts the punch in the golf shot.

-Jack Burke, Sr.

THE GOLFER HAS MORE ENEMIES than any other athlete. He has fourteen clubs in his bag, all of them different; eighteen holes to play, all of them different, every week; and all around him are sand, trees, grass, water, wind, and 143 other players. In addition, the game is 50% mental, so his biggest enemy is himself.

-Dan Jenkins

PEBBLE BEACH AND CYPRESS POINT make you want to play golf, they're such interesting and enjoyable layouts. Spyglass Hill — that's different; that makes you want to go fishing.

-Jack Nicklaus

TAKING MORE THAN TWO PUTTS to get down on a lightning-fast, steeply sloped green is no embarrassment unless you had to hit a wedge between the putts.

-Mulligan's Laws

SOME OF THE PLAYERS think it's an illegal aid, that I just aim it at the ground, make my turn around it, and follow through.

-Larry Laoretti
On his ever-present cigar

THIS HOLE IS HARDER than trigonometry.

-Hubert Green
On the ninth hole at Pebble Beach

IF A LOT OF PEOPLE GRIPPED a knife and fork like they do a golf club, they'd starve to death.

-Sam Snead

WE SPEAK OF eyeball-to-eyeball encounters between men great and small. Even more searching and revealing of character is the eyeball-to-golfball confrontation, whereby our most secret natures are mercilessly tested by a small, round, whitish object with no mind or will but with a very definite life of its own, and with whims perverse and beatific.

-John Stuart Martin

IF YOU ARE CAUGHT on a golf course during a storm and are afraid of lightning, hold up a 1-iron. Not even God can hit a 1-iron.

-Lee Trevino

IT WAS EASY, I missed a twenty-footer for a 12.

-Arnold Palmer
*When asked how he managed
to make a 13 on one hole
at the 1961 Los Angeles Open*

NOBODY EVER SWUNG a golf club too slowly.

-Bobby Jones

GOWF IS A WAY o' makin' a man naked. I would say tha' nowhere does a man go so naked as he does before a discernin' eye dressed for gowf.

-Peter McNaughton
Golf in the Kingdom *by Michael Murphy*

THE WORST CLUB in my bag is my brain.

-Chris Perry

GOLF AND SEX are about the only things you can enjoy without being good at.

-Jimmy Demaret

A GOLF COURSE IS the epitome of all that is purely transitory in the universe, a space not to dwell in, but to get over as quickly as possible.

-Jean Giraudoux

LIKE LIFE, GOLF CAN BE humbling. However, little good comes from brooding about mistakes we've made. The next shot, in golf or in life, is the big one.

-Grantland Rice

Yes, a man's style o' play and his swing certainly reflect the state of his soul. Ye take the ones who always under-club. The man who wants to think he's stronger than he is. D' ye ken anybody like that? Think about the rest of his habits. Is he always short o' the hole? Then there are the ones who are always owerclubbin' and landin' on the next tee. It's an X-ray of the soul, this game o gowf. I knew a married fellow from

London who kept a girl goin' here in town, a real captain's paradise. Well, damned if he didn't keep two scorecards for a round, one for the first nine and one for the second. And changed his balls for the second nine too, just like he did in real life. I wonder which scorecard he showed to his wife?

-Shivas Irons
Golf in the Kingdom *by Michael Murphy*

GOLF IS NOT one of those occupations in which you soon learn your level. There is no shape nor size of body, no awkwardness nor ungainliness, which puts good golf beyond one's reach. There are good golfers with spectacles, with one eye, with one leg, even with one arm. None but the absolutely blind need despair. It is not the youthful tyro alone who has cause to hope. Beginners in middle age have become great, and, more wonderful still, after years of patient duffering, there may be a rift in the clouds. Some pet vice which has been clung to as a virtue may be abandoned, and the fifth-class player burst upon the world as a medal winner. In golf, whilst there is life there is hope.

-Sir Walter Simpson

READING A GREEN IS LIKE reading the small type in a contract. If you don't read them with painstaking care, you are likely to be in trouble.

-Claude Hamilton

NEVER WASH YOUR BALL on the tee of a water hole.

-Mulligan's Laws

THE BRAIN CONTROLS the mind.

The mind controls the body.

The body controls the club.

-Mike Hebron
PGA Master Professional

Golf IS THE ONLY 'SPORT' where the object is to play as little as possible.

-Charles G. McLoughlin

Trouble ONCE BEGUN at this hole may never come to an end till the card is torn into a thousand fragments.

-Bernard Darwin
On the 11th hole at St. Andrews (1910)

I HAVE NEVER BEEN ABLE to see more rolls and bumps in a minute than I could in five seconds.

-Bobby Jones
On reading greens

MY GOLFING PAY ZIGGY says that our problem — mine, his, every hacker's problem — is not that we are inherently bad golfers; it's that we are inherently bad people, and therefore unable to play good golf. It's an interesting twist on Original Sin, and I think Zig may be on to something. If you think of the Garden of Eden as a golf course, then the snake becomes a two iron and the apple a golf ball. It would explain a lot.

-Glen Waggoner

PRACTICE TEE: THE PLACE where golfers go to convert a nasty hook into a wicked slice.

-Henry Beard and Roy McKie

To APPROACH THE HOLE remains the ultimate object in the game. Once the round is under way, the business in hand becomes that of getting results. Nothing else matters.

-Bobby Jones

GOLF ACTS AS a corrective against sinful pride. I attribute the insane arrogance of the later Roman emperors almost entirely to the fact that, never having played a round of golf, they never knew that strange chastening humility which is engendered by a topped chip shot.

-P. G. Wodehouse

MANY LIKE IT, most respect it, and all fear it.

-Bernard Darwin
On the Road Hole at St. Andrews

THE GOLF SWING is like sex. You can't be thinking about the mechanics of the act while you're performing.

-Dave Hill

MY HANDICAP? Woods and irons.

-Chris Codiroli

GOLF IS A GAME of blows and weapons. In order that the game continue we must make amends for every single act of destruction. In a golf club everyone knows the player who does not replace his divot. One can guess how he leads the rest of his life.

-Shivas Irons
Golf in the Kingdom *by Michael Murphy*

WILLIS' RULE OF GOLF: You can't lose an old golf ball.

-John Willis

GOLF HAS SOME DRAWBACKS. It is possible, by too much of it, to destroy the mind . . . For the golfer, Nature loses her significance. Larks, the casts of worms, the buzzing of bees, and even children are hateful . . . Rain comes to be regarded solely in its relation to the putting greens; the daisy is detested, botanical specimens are but 'hazards', twigs 'break clubs'. Winds cease to be east, south, west or north. They are ahead, behind, sideways, and sky is bright or dark, according to the state of the game.

-Sir Walter Simpson (1887)

BAD GOLF IS PLAYED with the shoulders and the body; good golf is played with the hands.

-Gene Sarazen

GOLFERS AS A RULE are an exceptionally honest race of men, but uncertain arithmetic is occasionally encountered on the green. 'I aim to tell the truth,' said one; 'Well, you are a very bad shot,' was the reply.

-Henry E. Howland
Scribner's Magazine (1895)

IF I AM ASKED WHICH is my favourite course, I give my answer unhesitatingly — the Old Course at St. Andrews. I think it is the best, and if I have got to play a match which is really of some importance, that is where I want to play it. St. Andrews has got a character and features that you find nowhere else. What I like about it is this, that you may play a very good shot there and find yourself in a very bad place. That is the real game of golf. I don't want everything levelled and smoothed away so that by no possible chance can your ball take an unlucky turn in a direction you don't like. People think and talk too much about 'fairness'.

-George Duncan

GOLF IS AN OPEN EXHIBITION of over-
whelming ambition, courage deflated
by stupidity, skill soured by a whiff of
arrogance. These humiliations are the
essence of golf.

-Alistair Cooke

AN AMATEUR GOLFER is one who plays
for honor — in my mind, that's tougher
than playing for money.

-Willie Turnesa
1938 U.S. Amateur champion

PLAYING GOLF IS A PRIVILEGE, not
a sentence.

-Harvey Penick

GOLF IS MORE EXCITING than racing, cards, speculation, or matrimony. Golf gives no margin: Either you win or you fail. You cannot hedge; you cannot bluff; you cannot give a stop-order; you cannot jilt. One chance is given you, and you hit or miss. There is nothing more rigid in life. And it is the ultra and extreme rigidity that makes golf so intensely interesting.

-Arnold Haultain

I SAY THIS WITHOUT ANY reservations whatsoever: It is impossible to outplay an opponent you cannot outthink.

-Lawson Little

CADDIES ARE A BREED of their own. If you shoot sixty-six, they say 'Man, we shot sixty-six!' But go out and shoot seventy-seven, and they say, 'Hell, he shot seventy-seven!'

-Lee Trevino

NERVES ARE LIKE some diseases: Some people are prone to them, others are not.

-Gary Player

I CAN STILL SEE HIM marching up the hill toward us, shoulders slightly hunched, head thrust forward, shirttail hanging out. That walk, that look, have been so much a part of golf for so long that it's easy to forget that they were once new. Back then, pro golfers looked like our fathers. Not Palmer. Palmer looked like your best friend's older brother, the one who had the '55 stick-shift Olds and who would sometimes let you hang out with him on Friday night.

-Glen Waggoner
On Arnold Palmer

PERHAPS THE BEST WAY of curing yourself of the tendency to become irritable
and morose when you are playing badly
is to pull yourself up and think how
objectionable and ridiculous other people
look when they are in the same state.

-H. J. Whigham
The Common Sense of Golf (1910)

GO OUT WITH A DEFINITE purpose and
stay with your work only so long as that
purpose remains definite. If the purpose
is achieved, go home and give your
muscles and your head a rest. Nothing
can be gained by dithering with your swing
after it has been once straightened out.

-Bobby Jones
On practice

GOLF RECAPITULATES EVOLUTION, it is a microcosm of the world, a projection of all our hopes and fears.

-Adam Greene
Golf in the Kingdom *by Michael Murphy*

THAT'S CALLED 'Body Spanish.'

-Bob Murphy
Watching Chi Chi Rodriguez
coax in a putt

THE FIRST TIME I SAW Jack Nicklaus in person, he reminded me of the Alamo — neither is anywhere as big as I had expected.

-Glen Waggoner

WE CAN HAVE NO ASSURANCE after hitting seventeen fine tee shots, that the eighteenth will not be disgraceful. These are the uncertainties the golfer accepts as parts of the game, and indeed loves it all the more because of them.

-Bobby Jones

LET'S FACE IT, 95 PERCENT of this game is mental. A guy plays lousy golf, he doesn't need a pro, he needs a shrink.

-Tom Murphy

THE GREATEST OF CHAMPIONS have all been ex-chokers.

-Peter Dobereiner

UNDER AN ASSUMED name.

-Tommy Bolt
When asked by an amateur
partner how he should play
a particularly difficult shot

THE DEVOTED GOLFER is an anguished soul who has learned a lot about putting just as an avalanche victim has learned a lot about snow.

-Dan Jenkins

PRACTICING IS MY MEDITATION. Some golfers like to fish and others read. I hit golf balls.

-Lee Trevino

YE TRY TOO HARD and ye think too much. Why don't ye go wi' yer pretty swing? Let the nothingness into yer shots.

-Shivas Irons
Golf in the Kingdom *by Michael Murphy*

BEN HOGAN PLAYED a golf course the way a locomotive runs down a railroad track, making only scheduled stops.

-Jerry Tarde

GOLF IS NOT A FUNERAL, although both can be very sad affairs.

-Bernard Darwin

THE MORE I STUDIED the Old Course, the more I loved it, and the more I loved it, the more I studied it. So that I came to feel that it was, for me, the most favorable meeting ground possible for an important contest. I felt that my knowledge of the course enabled me to play it with patience and restraint, until she might exact her toll from my adversary who might treat her with less respect and understanding.

-Bobby Jones
On the Old Course at St. Andrews

Out OF A POSSIBLE seventy-five million, there are less than a million people in this country who play golf. At least seventy-four million are willfully depriving themselves of one of the most certain methods of attaining health and happiness. If you were assured that without imbibing any new-fangled religion and regardless of all the the new dietists and doctors who fill the human body full of parasites for the sake of destroying other parasites, you could not only add twenty years to the normal span of life, but secure in the present at least one good day out of seven by the simple process of swinging a golf club, would you not rush to the nearest golf links and begin to take lessons from the local professional?

-H. J. Whigham
The Common Sense of Golf (1910)

CHOOSE A 7-IRON or a 6-iron, whichever one you feel the most confidence in, and use it for 80% of all your full-swing practice. The reason for this is I want you to develop faith in your golf swing. The best way to learn to trust your swing is by practicing your swing with a club you trust.

-Harvey Penick

ANYONE SLICING THE BALL has reached the top of his game. The harder he hits, the more it will slice.

-Jack Burke, Sr.

THE FUNDAMENTAL PROBLEM with golf is that every so often, no matter how lacking you may be in the essential virtues required of a steady player, the odds are that one day you will hit the ball straight, hard, and out of sight. This is the essential frustration of this excruciating sport. For when you've done it once, you make the fundamental error of asking yourself why you can't do it all the time. The answer to this question is simple: The first time was a fluke.

-Colin Bowles

My FIRST THOUGHT on watching pros go through long, tedious practice drills was similar to my reaction on seeing lean, hard, obviously fit people running in the park. If you're in such good shape, why run so much? If you can play golf as well as you do, why spend so much time on boring practice drills? And then it dawned on me: Maybe there was a connection.

-Glen Waggoner

Just KEEP LAUGHING and smiling.

-Walter Hagen
When asked how to deal with the strong, cold winds at the British Open

ONE DAY HE SHOT A NINETY, yes, a ninety, my friends, and laughed and complimented me all the way. Had a grand time, he did, never lookin' back at par, never panickin' or cursin', just steady through it a', the same as he always is. And that I say is the mark o' a brave and holy man, that he can retreat like that from par without a whimper. I've never forgotten that holy round, the memory o' it haunts me still and settles me after many a rotten hole.

-Evan Tyree
On Shivas Irons
Golf in the Kingdom *by Michael Murphy*

IN GOLF YOUR STRENGTHS and weaknesses will always be there. If you could improve your weaknesses, you would improve your game. The irony is that people prefer to practice their strengths.

-Harvey Penick

LET THE BALL GET IN THE WAY of the swing instead of making the ball the object.

-Jack Burke, Sr.

THE NEXT one.

-Ben Hogan
When asked what is the most important shot in golf

Do ye know any other game where ye roam so far and wide to reach such a tiny goal? Why do we submit to such a thing?

-Shivas Irons
Golf in the Kingdom *by Michael Murphy*

At my best, I never came close to the golf Byron Nelson shoots.

-Bobby Jones

Whatever you do, partner, keep it low.

-Chi Chi Rodriguez
When asked by an extremely nervous pro-am partner how to play a putt

IT'S HARD TO TELL whether Americans have become such liars because of golf or the income tax.

-Will Rogers

WALTER HAGEN WAS THE FIRST player I knew that earned $1 million from golf, and of course he spent it, too. Sam Snead earned $1 million, too — and he saved $2 million.

-Fred Corcoran

VERY EARLY IN OUR TIME together I try to get my pupils to hit the ball hard, even with the short irons. I believe if you start off in the game hitting the ball easy, you generally will keep it up. Your muscles learn the slow pace. You will always lack distance. Sometimes it takes longer to unlearn than it does to learn.

-Harvey Penick

TO ME, GOLF IS AN INEXHAUSTIBLE subject. I cannot imagine that anyone might ever write every word that needs to be written about the golf swing.

-Bobby Jones

We cannot refrain for the life of us from closing our remarks on golfing without some expression of our intense attachment to it . . . Golf, thou art a gentle spirit; we owe thee much!

-H. B. Farnie (1857)

INDEX